COVERED BRIDGES
In Illinois, Iowa and Wisconsin

by
LESLIE C. SWANSON

ACKNOWLEDGEMENTS

This new edition marks the 26th anniversary of the original issue of this book, which was the first work of its kind in the tri-state area. In getting together this material we are indebted to many people, who are dedicated to the task of preserving the covered bridges.

Among those who have contributed information or pictures or who have assisted in other ways are the following:

Illinois — Rep. Ralph Stephenson, Moline; Earl Ellamaker, Sterling; Don Bright, Rock Island; Mrs. Cora Watkins, Lockport; I. F. Plagge, Deerfield; several district offices of the Illinois State Highway Division, the Illinois Department of Conservation, the State Historical Society, and Dorothy Golden, Petersburg, IL.

Iowa — Clee Crawford of Winterset; the late D. M. Ludwig of Tiffin; Leslie Ritchie, Knoxville; Mrs. Mayme Hughes, Hamilton; Al Erhardt and Dr. L. A. Meder, Elkader; Leslie Graversen, Plymouth; Grace Alderson and Gladys Kenneally, Strawberry Point; Mrs. Fred Hartsook, Spencer; the Winterset Chamber of Commerce; and Polk County Department of Conservation.

Wisconsin — Wayne L. Gibson, Superior; Chester Czynszak, Milwaukee; Lois Williams, Eau Claire; Mrs. Dorothy McCarthy, Portage; James King, River Falls; Mrs. Sarah L. Willson, Baraboo; Byron Tuckwood, Boscobel; the Wisconsin Historical Society; State Highway Commission; Virgil Jackson, Beaver Dam; and Carel C. Koch, Jr., Madison.

Also assisting were librarians in all three states, many county historical societies and numerous covered bridge fans who have called our attention to recently erected private spans.

Illustration credits — Frontispiece, Vicki Swanson Wassenhove; Amnicon bridge photo, Lois Williams; Boscobel bridge photo, Wisconsin State Historical Society; sketch of Red Mill bridge, Gloria Janetski; Red Mill bridge and Imes bridge photos by Carel C. Koch, Jr.;

ILLUSTRATIONS

No. 1 — The Red bridge near Princeton, IL.
No. 2 — Wolf bridge near Douglas and Gilson, IL.
No. 3 — Illinois map of old and new covered bridges.
No. 4 — Rebuilt Henderson Creek span near Oquawka, IL.
No. 5 — Greenbush bridge in Warren County, IL.
No. 6 — Sangamon River bridge in Lake of Woods park.
No. 7 — Thompson Mill span on Kaskaskia River, IL.
No. 8 — Little Mary's River bridge at Chester, IL.
No. 9 — Sugar Creek bridge near Glenarm, IL.
No. 10 — Spring Creek bridge near Springfield, IL.
No. 11 — Restored covered bridge at Petersburg, IL.
No. 12 — Iowa map of old and new covered bridges.
No. 13 — Cutler span in Winterset, IA.
No. 14 — McBride bridge north of Winterset, IA.
No. 15 — Hogback bridge near Winterset, IA.
No. 16 — Cedar bridge near Winterset, IA.
No. 17 — Roseman bridge southwest of Winterset, IA.
No. 18 — Holliwell span southeast of Winterset, IA.
No. 19 — Imes bridge in St. Charles, IA.
No. 20 — North Skunk River span near Delta, IA.
No. 21 — Hammond bridge west of Marysville, IA.
No. 22 — New bridge along Shell Rock River, IA.
No. 23 — Owens bridge in Polk County, IA, park.
No. 24 — Covered bridge at Hamilton, IL.
No. 25 — Boscobel, WI, covered bridge.
No. 26 — Famous span at Mederville, IA.
No. 27 — New bridge at State Park near Cassville, WI.
No. 28 — Red Mill bridge near Waupaca, WI.
No. 29 — Amnicon River span near Superior, WI.
No. 30 — Cedar Creek bridge near Cedarburg, WI.
No. 31 — Marysville, IA, covered bridge.
No. 32 — Knoxville, IA, span in the Wilcox Game Reserve.
No. 33 — Bridge at a city park at the southwest edge of Knoxville, IA.
No. 34 — New DuPage River span at Naperville.
No. 35 — Red Mill covered bridge at Waupaca.

TABLE OF CONTENTS

CHAPTER I — **History and Development** — Three states on fringe of covered bridge building belt — How history figured in their development — Superhighways and the historic landmarks — Many new spans.

CHAPTER II — **Legends, Folk Lore and Notes** — Spooks, lovers and legends — Kissing bridges or tunnels of love — The haunted bridges — Why the bridges were covered.

CHAPTER III — **Illinois Bridges** — State's total of covered bridges growing — The framing of legislation — State rehabilitates some spans — New bridges erected.

CHAPTER IV — **Iowa Bridges** — Winterset, the heart of covered bridge country — All near superhighways — Beautiful new bridge along Shellrock River — The forgotten core of covered bridges.

CHAPTER V — **Wisconsin Bridges** — Famed bridges of Wisconsin River at Boscobel, Portage and Bridgeport — New spans at Cassville and Waupaca — Spectacular Scenery at Amnicon River bridge — Number increasing.

CHAPTER I — HISTORY AND DEVELOPMENT

The tri-state area of Illinois, Iowa and Wisconsin shared in a great wave of covered bridge building which enveloped most of the eastern half of the U.S. About 15,000 to 20,000 of the covered spans were built in the nation and approximately 345 of that number were erected in the three states of our subject area. Illinois led the region with approximately 200, a late historical census showed 85 once existed in Iowa and 60 more were located in Wisconsin.

Practically all of the historic bridges were built in the Nineteenth Century as the nation pushed westward. The belt of timbered structures stretched from New England, through the Middle Atlantic States, into much of the south and part of the mid-west, terminating in the upper reaches of the Mississippi Valley. The tri-state area was thus on the outer fringes of the regions reached by the pioneer builders.

America's era of covered bridge building began at Philadelphia in 1805 and extended in full swing for much of the 19th century. Hundreds of the picturesque structures were built in the Quaker State and elsewhere in the east and hundreds more were erected to the west in Ohio and Indiana. Illinois, Iowa and Wisconsin came next as the trend pushed westward, bringing the tri-state area into the growth and development years of the nation.

The three states were on the crossroads of history in early America. This was the land made famous by the French Voyageurs, the fur traders, and trappers, the Indian fighters, the pathfinders who blazed the first trails through the wilderness, the pioneer river boat men and the settlers. Sitting astride a vast portion of the Upper Mississippi Valley system, the territory's waterways played an important role in the economic growth which led to statehood. The thousands of miles of waterways became broad highways as the early settlers moved into the region. In the early decades of the 19th century settlements and mills sprang up, wagon trails jabbed into the interior and stagecoach lines made their appearance.

Fording places on the many streams were frequently flooded and an early need arose for bridges at key points. The first bridges thus played a vital role in opening vast new stretches of territory for settlement and development. The story of the covered bridge building in the tri-state area is therefore intricately interwoven with the 19th century history of the mid-west. The early builders left their mark in many historic structures still standing, a number of surviving old mills, the covered bridges and several hundred miles of old canals and locks.

Illinois, Iowa and Wisconsin were somewhat overlooked for many years as "covered bridge states." This tourism potentiality has come to the front only in recent years. It was brought about by persistent restoration efforts, the building of many new covered bridges, and a general resurgence of sentiment favoring these treasured symbols of our historic past.

Today there is an encouraging total of 70 covered bridges existing in the three states. This figure is debatable and the accepted total would hinge upon the yardstick used in assembling the statistics. From a historical point of view you would consider 19 authentic covered bridges in existence with 11 in Iowa, six in Illinois and one in Wisconsin. But if you take into account structures built since 1916 you would find four more in Wisconsin, two additional in Illinois and two in Iowa. If the count is widened further to include many new smaller bridges the count would be Illinois, 37; Iowa, 18; and Wisconsin 15.

A record number of generally smaller type spans were erected in an unprecedented wave of such construction in the decade of the 1970's. Such spans found many new uses such as private property, entrances to housing developments, country clubs, trail ride routes, pedestrian foot traffic in crossings in parks and zoos, and such. Much of this construction may have been encouraged by the frequent appearance of covered bridges on television commercials and shows.

The national total of standing historical covered bridges at this writing is approximately 950. Pennsylvania is the leader with over 200; Ohio has 120 and Indiana, 105. Other states high on the list include Vermont, 100; New Hampshire, 64; and Oregon, 60. Parke County in Indiana, still has 35 bridges, the heaviest concentration in the entire world.

Many of the states in the mid-west are entirely without covered bridges. Missouri has four (Minnesota has one land-locked bridge in a park at Zumbrota), but the last roofs over rivers disappeared in Minnesota and Kansas some years ago. Other plains states and most of the Rocky Mountain area were never reached by the covered bridge builders. The coming of the Iron age and subsequent developments of concrete revolutionized the methods of bridge building before these states were extensively settled.

One separate core of covered bridge building later developed in the three Pacific coast states where a number of beautiful structures still stand. Much of the construction in the western states came early in the present century.

Covered bridges are considered a typical American product although the idea for such structures no doubt came from Europe. Some sturdily built roofed structures have existed in Switzerland for centuries. Some of them date back to medieval times. The oldest known covered Timber bridges were the Chapel bridge and the "Dance of Death" bridge built in Lucerne, Switzerland in 1333. History records the next famous bridges as the Reichenau and Shaffhausen spans, erected in 1756 and 1758 by two Swiss carpenters, Johannese and Hans Ulrich. Hundreds of covered bridges were subsequently built in other European countries. Most of them are found in three countries — Switzerland with slightly over 100, Austria with 120 and West Germany with 130. Many of these bridges have made fascinating camera subjects for American visitors on summer tours in recent years.

The early American covered bridge builders borrowed somewhat from the work of their counterparts in the Old World but in the space of a few years American carpenters, engineers and inventors put their talents to work in a vast construction program. More than a dozen truss styles, all distinctly American, emerged and thousands of men found work in this steadily growing industry. It is estimated that between 200 and 400 covered bridges were being built annually in the U.S. in some of the more productive years between 1840 and 1890.

Not all of the various trusses, developed in the east, will be found in a study of covered bridges in the tri-state area. The three most common ones noted here are the Burr, the Howe and the Town lattice truss. The Burr plan consisted of a huge arch arrangement invented by Theodore Burr of Torrington, CT. It was patented in 1817 and well preserved samples of it are found in many states. Ithiel Town's plan was a lattice type truss, which resembles the criss-cross arrangement you might find in a garden fence. It was patented in 1820. William Howe's truss, which was not patented until 1849, was the first to use iron in part of his setup. His plan consisted of a combination of timbers and iron, fitted together in the form of timber diagonals with vertical iron tension rods.

Illinois builders generally favored the Burr and Howe trusses; Iowa had a predominance of the lattice truss and Wisconsin's oldest bridge at Cedarburg also is this classification. Other well known trusses which are found more commonly in eastern states include the following: Palmer, Long, Paddleford, Kingpost, Queenpost, and Smith.

The achievements of the nation's covered bridge builders and the integral part they played in developing a great nation are a saga of engineering triumph. Modern day engineers gaze in awe and wonderment as they examine the work of the men of over a century ago. The early engineers and carpenters overcame all sorts of obstacles, laboring without nails, spikes, bolts or modern tools of craftsmen. The bridges were fitted together and held in place by tree nails (wooden pegs) which were pounded into position. Material was often scarce but the early day builders made the most of what they had.

They never had the benefit of scientific methods for calculating bridge stresses and strength and weight loads. Their only known formula was to build a bridge "more than strong" enough to carry the loads they were called upon to sustain. Their accuracy is attested by modern day trucks with loads of up to six and eight tons, still rumbling over some of the century-old structures. The bridges stand as a fitting monument to the 19th century builders who entered the undeveloped mid-west and left a much improved land.

A good share of the nation's surviving covered bridges are still in use. Vehicular traffic is possible over about one half of the covered bridges in the tri-state area and the remainder is open to foot traffic or in some cases, carriage, bridle path or bicycle use.

The bridges in our subject area are some of the most conveniently located in the entire U.S. Whereas some bridges in other states are found on little used back roads, mountain trails or in generally remote areas, all of the timbered crossings here are fairly close to paved highways. Well traveled gravel or black top roads lead right up to and usually beyond them. In subsequent chapters the author will outline possible interesting two or three-day tours for each of the three states.

Developments in recent years have brought some drastic changes in the covered bridge visiting prospects. The expanding network of superhighways in particular has contributed greatly to the ease of accessibility of the bridges and has lessened considerably the amount of time required to tour these landmarks. Some of the bridges are practically right on the nation's busiest thoroughfares now.

The strange contrast of the sharp pace of modern life and the leisurely tempo of a century ago is vividly emphasized as you travel about the midwest today. One moment you may be breezing along the expressway at 55 miles an hour and a few minutes later you may find yourself communing with nature and the past at a covered bridge just a short distance off the paved route. This abrupt change of pace might prove momentarily startling but you will adjust readily to the transition from the new back to the old and incidentally thoroughly enjoy it. As one Illinois legislator once commented to the author, "Perhaps we should just slow down and look around." This remark was made during the framing of legislation to save Illinois' covered bridges.

The Red bridge near Princeton, IL, the Glenarm span near Springfield, IL, and the Imes span in Iowa are all within a short distance of new expressways. On one occasion the writer, armed with a stop watch, found it took slightly more than two minutes from the superhighway, on through the cloverleaf interchange and on to the portal of the Red covered bridge a mile and a half away. All of Iowa's historic covered bridges are located fairly close to Superhighways Nos. 80 and 35 and each can be reached in not more than a half hour or less of driving.

Other bridges only a few miles from new four-lane highways include the Wolf bridge over the Spoon River in Illinois and the new Sangamon River bridge near Mahomet, IL.

Another interesting development in recent years has been a new era of constructing timbered bridges. This revival has been sizable enough to attract much attention and publicity for the hobby. In an era in which we are concerned with preserving the bridges we still have, it was quite surprising to many observers to find a resurgence of sentiment in favor of building new covered spans.

Dozens of private covered bridges have been built and there have been several full scale spans erected which rival anything built during the 19th century. The most notable examples of new bridges include the Sangamon River bridge in Illinois, erected in 1965; the Bunker Hill Road bridge, erected near Hereford, MD, in 1963, to replace a span which had burned; the new bridge built at Woodstock, VT, in 1968; a new span erected the same year along the Shell Rock River near Rock Falls, IA, and a new bridge erected at East Pepperell, MA, in 1963.

These full scale spans, plus the newly-erected private bridges are a credit to the communities, states and individuals who erected them. They are considered apart now from the historical bridges of the 19th century but as time goes on they will attain stature among America's historical buildings. These picturesque little spans have made a worthwhile contribution to the hobby as a whole. Although they do not attain rank as timbered structures with a historical background, they do attract many visitors and help to make the public more covered bridge-conscious. They are also given recognition amongst the world-wide count in the book, *World Guide to Covered Bridges*.

Other covered bridges with more practical purposes have been erected in various parks. One such covered bridge is the span, erected in 1962, by the Wisconsin State Historical Society in the Nelson Dewey State Park near Cassville. Another is the covered bridge serving a small railroad in the Niabi Zoo park, south of Moline, IL. These new arrivals help to preserve the image of the hobby and they gratify tourists, who appear enchanted as they examine such symbols of yesteryear.

Much has been learned in the past three decades in regard to covered bridge preservation. The charm and beauty of our historical buildings has not always been recognized. Almost 75 per cent of our original stand of covered bridges in the U.S. had vanished before many people became concerned about the "alarming disappearance of this phase of our American heritage."

The first big task was to overcome public apathy as the bridges were lost one by one. Many fates were suffered by the disappearing spans. Some on by-passed roads were simply condemned and forgotten before they finally died of neglect. Others crashed into creeks or rivers when over-loaded; many were wiped out by floods; vandals wrecked many of them; and hundreds more were simply razed in the name of progress and economy. Organized efforts of several covered bridge societies, state and county historical groups, interested individuals and legislators all had much influence in saving many of the covered bridges still standing today. Without the work of these groups a bare few hundred covered spans would still be in existence.

It has been conservatively estimated that about half of the existing covered bridges owe their present life to the work of such groups, who refuse to permit any structure to die if there is any possible way of saving it. In many cases bridges have been saved merely by moving them to new locations or simply building new roads around them. All forms of Americana share in the new trend to preserve historic mementoes of our momentous past. Old Mills, old canals, ghost towns, round barns, Indian mounds, and other historic sites are coming in for new hobby attention as rapidly expanding population becomes more mobile and finds more time on its hands.

Covered bridges are much like many forms of Americana whose true heritage value was not recognized until the threat of extinction became apparent. Any article or building must become scarce before it becomes classified as a "collector's item." Tourism is annually becoming a bigger business in the U.S. and covered bridges fit admirably into the campaign to "Discover America." Americana in all its forms is one gigantic focal point in this drive and there is much to discover if you want to go covered bridge hunting and exploring.

CHAPTER II — LEGENDS, FOLK LORE AND NOTES

Covered bridges have many legends and traditions surrounding them. They are actually something of a still living legend and a tangible link with a by-gone era, when the nation was in its formative years.

The words, "covered bridges," themselves ring with a grandeur which is kept alive by the hardy survivors still in use. Take a stroll through any in the three states today and you will be walking right back into history and harking back to the "good old days," grandpa so fondly recalls. The shadowed interior will be dark and cool, the aged planks will rumble as cars move through and you will marvel at the carvings of all descriptions on the dusty walls.

Covered bridges present an intriguing combination of quaintness, charm, beauty and romance with plenty of history and legend mixed in. The romantic side brought the spans the name of "kissing bridges," an appellation which has existed for over a century. "Tunnels of love," is another name which was attached to them. Many a bashful swain finally mustered enough courage to steal the first kiss from his lady fair after entering the darkened bridge. Sometimes these scenes of tenderness and love would be interrupted by hecklers, who lay in wait in the rafters to spy on such lovers' trysts.

Many of the young lovers descended from their buggies to carve their initials amid heart-shaped symbols on the inner part of the bridge's siding or in the truss. This custom is still continued and each year finds a new crop of carvings, dates, names and addresses, often alongside some objectionable matter. The carvings on the wall support the legends of the bridges serving as trysting places. As you wander through the bridge scanning the initials you wonder what stories they tell, who the people were and where they are today. The bridge, a somber witness to time, holds the secret. Several generations have come and gone since the bridges were built a century or more ago but the practice of carving initials goes merrily on. Dates in the 1900's, the roaring twenties and more up-to-date fresher carvings are found side by side. If there is a generation gap it is not evident in the covered bridge carvings.

Missing from the bridges today, however, is the wealth of signs and advertising matter which once decorated the inside of every span. Only fragments may be found of the handbills and posters which advertised a wide list of things including chewing tobacco, cure-all patent medicines, political events, county fairs, political candidates, etc. County and state authorities now frown on the posting of such advertising and any such activity might result in a fine. Covered bridges were a popular place for posting such literature in the old days as the roof gave the paper and cardboard protection from the rain, snow and the wind.

One conspicuous but out-dated sign does remain on two of the Illinois spans, the Red bridge near Princeton and the Henderson Creek span near Oquawka. One of them reads as follows: FIVE DOLLAR FINE FOR LEADING OR DRIVING ANY BEAST FASTER THAN A WALK OR DRIVING MORE THAN THIRTY HEAD OF CATTLE, MULES OR HORSES AT A TIME ON OR

ACROSS THIS BRIDGE.

The bridges were built sturdy enough to carry such loads but it was feared that the rhythmic beat of too many horses or cattle would throw too much stress and strain on the timbers. Two or more horses moving in step together, were considered more of a peril to a bridge than an unusually heavy load.

The bridges came to have many uses. Children often converted them into playgrounds. On a rainy day they frequently became baseball diamonds despite the narrow confines. Campers and fishermen used them as shelters on rainy nights as there was very little night traffic in the old days. The landmarks proved a fertile field for magazine and newspaper cartoonists who depicted the bridges as veritable tunnels of love, poking fun at the participants in all sorts of situations. Some of cartoons have become classics and are frequently reprinted in covered bridge literature.

Numerous jokes about the activities of lovers on the bridges also were inevitable. Our favorite story, one which we have re-told many times, concerns a young couple out for a Sunday drive in a buggy. When a covered bridge suddenly loomed ahead, the young swain, with a flair for the dramatic, explained: "Oooooo, we are going into one of those dark and haunted bridges, aren't you scared?" "No, not a bit," was the reply, "just make sure you take that stogie out of your mouth."

An aura of mystery surrounded some of the bridges. Beside being a rendezvous for lovers, some of the bridges in remote areas, gained a reputation of being haunted or bandit-infested. Wild tales of ghosts, weird noises and other strange happenings were frequently reported and it took a mighty intrepid youngster to walk through the black interiors after sundown.

Most of the bridges were without windows and a moonlight night would convert the interior into a contrasty, impenetrable darkness. A youngster, gingerly stepping through a darkened bridge, could imagine all sorts of spooks or weird things ready to pounce upon him from the rafters. A forbidding place at night, a covered bridge was no place for any one with a too vivid imagination. Once a ghost had been "sighted," the eerie tales and strange happenings became more weird as they were re-told. Bats fluttering about, gleams of moonlight streaking through tiny cracks or knotholes, screeching of owls and the howling of coyotes, could frighten any youngster and even some of the adults. There was only one reassuring thing for a youngster. He was quite sure there were no witches about as he had frequently heard such creatures were generally credited with being "afraid of water."

One of the so-called "haunted bridges" is the Roseman span, one of six such historic landmarks in Madison County, IA. The legend surrounding this bridge developed from a historic man hunt after a jail break in Winterset, the county seat, in 1892. The hunted escapee had been spotted in the vicinity of the Roseman span and two well armed posses converged on their prey from different directions. With his escape cut off, the man ran into the bridge, gave a horrible cry of anguish and then simply vanished. The posses rushed onto the bridge and there was nothing there. In the confusion that ensued with vigilantes pouring onto the bridge from both sides, one of the posse members was accidentally wounded.

It was finally concluded that the escapee had vaulted up the trusswork and had burst through a hole in the roof. Supporting this tale today are still visible repair marks on the roof. This incident contributed to the legend that the bridge is haunted. On fog-shrouded nights there have been frequent reports by fishermen of wild and raucous laughter and hurried footsteps coming from the bridge. These reports have kept alive the strange legend that the spirit of the missing man still haunts the bridge.

The Marysville bridge in Marion County, IA, was another span which gained a reputation as the site of strange nocturnal occurrences. The screeching of owls was believed to have caused several teams of horses to run away late at night. As the stories became more and more exaggerated they finally emerged as "armed robbery attempts." Many horses are high strung and excitable. In a strange, dark place such as a covered bridge it would not take much to cause a nervous animal to bolt.

Legend also relates that some Illinois covered bridges were used as a place to hide slaves during the days of the underground railroad. The story goes that the slaves were hidden up in the rafters during the day while the principal movement to new stations was made during the night.

The covered bridge's mixed image of legends, spooks, lovers and general tranquility was not always thus. War, violence, tragedy and bloodshed also entered the picture in somewhat isolated instances. During the Civil War covered bridges became the site of battles for river crossings and some of them were used as makeshift barracks. Stories were also related of one man being shot to death on a covered bridge in a case of mistaken identity in the dim light. A murderer was put to death on one bridge with the rafters serving as part of the scaffolding.

The bridges also have had a few fatal traffic accidents. A young man was killed when a team of horses ran away at a covered bridge in Illinois, another young farmer was killed near Avon, IL, when a very small covered bridge over a creek collapsed under the weight of a tractor, and two young brothers were killed one night when a tractor fell through the floor of a covered bridge over the Volga River near Elkader, IA.

A few bridges obtained an unsavory reputation as being definitely unsafe at night, when they served as hangouts for robbers, thugs and highwaymen. One such bridge was the span over the Chippewa River at Chippewa Falls, WI. The bridge was originally constructed without a roof which was added a few years later. The roof first led to complaints due to the lack of snow for the farmers' sleighs. Later the bridge became the site of several holdups, giving it the reputation of being a "robbers' roost." When the bridge finally burned down some years later the apparent incendiary blaze was hailed as a welcome relief to inhabitants of the area. Some considered it a colossal mistake to have built a covered bridge in the first place.

"Why were the bridges covered?" This question always comes up sooner or later when the author is interviewed on a television or radio program, or by a news reporter. Every casual observer will ask the same question. It is easy to explain the roof was added to protect the truss members from moisture. Wood, if exposed to the elements, would rot within a few years. The roof was the only protection available in the 19th century, long before the development of creosoted wood, moisture-resisting chemicals and other methods of treatment.

Early writers suggested many ridiculous theories in explaining the need for a roof. Some of them were as follows: A place to get out of the rain with a load of hay; a protective covering to keep horses from bolting at the sight of water; a cool place in the summer for resting your horses; and providing a barn-like appearance to encourage horses or a herd of cattle to move through.

There are other myths or misconceptions concerning covered bridges. To the casual observer the words "covered bridges" would be merely synonymous with New England. It has already been shown that Pennsylvania, Ohio and Indiana are the three principal covered bridge states and it also should be pointed out that Illinois and Iowa each have more of the historic landmarks than four of the states in New England. Another mistaken belief is the idea that the bridges date back to colonial times, whereas all of the existing spans in the U.S. today were built after 1805.

Interest in covered bridges has been growing by leaps and bounds in recent years. Thousands of tourists are going covered bridge hunting for the first time each year. A visit or a search for a covered bridge will give you an opportunity to do some exploring of historic places you may never have seen before. It's a good chance to pick up some history and enjoy some real country charm in the colorful mid-west.

Locating a covered bridge for the first time is always a thrilling experience. You will have an exhilarating feeling of anticipation as you know from your maps and directions that you are getting close to a covered bridge. You will observe the road slanting generally downward and you will be sure your objective is somewhere near as you pass into the valley of the river, creek or brook the bridge must cross.

Broad vistas of beautiful scenery usually unfold as every valley is entered. Your road may take a sweeping curve one way or the other, there may be a small intermediate incline to pass over, a jog to the left or right and then suddenly the bridge in all its glory and splendor comes into view, standing like a stately sentinel and guarding time and all the history of the scene it overlooks.

As you approach the bridge and walk through the portal you will have a strange feeling of turning back several generations of time, walking right back into the 19th century and coming face to face with a piece of our heritage.

When you pick a vantage point to photograph this landmark, you might pause and reconstruct the scene of yesteryear. You might half close your eyes and visualize a happy young couple in a buggy, slowing down Old Dobbin and stopping in the inner privacy of the bridge.

Another imaginary scene might be a winter wonderland of horses and a cutter with sleigh bells merrily ringing, the horses' hooves crunching the snow and clouds of vapor emitting from their mouths and nostrils. For many photographers and artists the most spectacular view is a snow-capped bridge, framed by a sparkling snow and over-hanging trees.

In summertime you can easily picture a farmer with a wagon, urging on his horses as they approach the bridge. He sharply cracks the reins at the backs of the horses if they show the slightest hesitancy to plunging into the barn-like structure. "Giddy-ap there!" he yells at them as the groaning and creaking rig rumbles into the now vigorously vibrating bridge. The loose planks and rhythmic rat-a-tat of the horses' hooves set up a reverberating rumble and roar which seem to shake the structure to its very bones. Just as the vibrations and crescendo reach their peaks, the horses burst through the opposite portal. The bridge suddenly becomes still and quiet again but another clatter develops as the horses go on and beyond amid a clippity-clop over the loose rock and hardened pieces of clay. The driver continues to cluck at them and down the road they go in a lingering cloud of dust with the echoes of the passage fading across the valley. This was all a part of the American scene in grandpa's day.

CHAPTER III — ILLINOIS' COVERED BRIDGES

Illinois has rapidly risen to prominence in recent years in the new-found role of being a "covered bridge" state. Developments on several fronts in recent decades have contributed to this new-found stature.

A number of covered bridges were built in an action-packed decade, another long forgotten bridge was discovered and completely restored, favorable legislation to save the remaining historic treasures was passed by the Illinois State Assembly and the State Highway Division has performed a noteworthy job of restoring them.

Illinois now counts 37 bridges of which 29 are small private spans or park type structures.

Illinois' proximity to Indiana, one of the three great covered bridge states, brought the territory into the scope of the timbered crossing building a few years ahead of Iowa and Wisconsin. After the turn of the century settlers converged on the area from the east and the south. They made their first homes along the many rivers, which provided an abundant supply of water and the principal means of transportation. Gradually they pushed into the interior plains, developing wagon trails and building bridges as they went along. Some of the earliest roofless bridges were crude contraptions. Stronger and better looking spans emerged as experienced covered bridge builders moved in from Indiana and Ohio.

As the state was cleared of Indians in the northern sectors the center of population gradually shifted. Illinois entered statehood in 1818 and grew rapidly as the then leading agricultural area of the expanding mid-west. By 1850 Illinois had also become an important lumber market, a development which figured in the building of roofs over the rivers.

Covered bridge building continued unabated in Illinois for several decades before the coming of the Iron Age brought this activity to almost a standstill about 1900. A good share was built along the two great interior watersheds, the Illinois River, which drains much of the state, and Rock River, which covers much of the northern and northwest corner. Five railroad bridges and 14 other spans were built on the Rock.

By 1900, it was estimated there were about 200 covered bridges in Illinois. The decline in number slowly began at the turn of the century. Approximately 80 per cent of the covered spans had disappeared by 1925 and in 1930 an unofficial count showed 27 were still standing. A magazine article, published in 1952, revealed that the count had dwindled to 16. By 1960, at the time of the original edition of this book, the count had sagged to a new low of nine. Two of the bridges were in a very shakey condition and without much repair work were doomed to go the way of many others.

Legislation toward saving the remaining historic spans was instituted in 1961, one year after the first edition of this book appeared. It all began when the author called at the office of State Rep. Ralph Stephenson in our home town of Moline and suggested that "legislative action of some sort be attempted looking toward preservation of the bridges." At that initial conference we were at first undecided on just what form of effective action might be taken and what might have a chance of being passed by the assembly. For years the matter of covered bridge preservation had been treated with complete apathy and appalling indifference.

One of the proposals was the creation of a state covered bridge commission but that idea was passed over in favor of a house measure, which was adopted March 7, 1961, just a few weeks after our initial conference.

The resolution, which was presented by Rep. Stephenson, was as follows:

"Whereas, covered bridges are fast becoming rare in Illinois, having dwindled to nine from an estimated 100 to 200 spans which once served the state;

"Whereas, these remaining bridges provide a link with the past which will be irreplaceable if they are destroyed; and

"Whereas, covered bridges and their surroundings are perfect sites for park and picnic grounds, and an ideal subject for photographers and artists, and

"Whereas, these structures of days gone by should be preserved as monuments to our pioneer forefathers who built our state; therefore, be it

RESOLVED, by the House of Representatives of the 72nd

General Assembly that this house strongly urges all highway officials of the State of Illinois and local road officials to take necessary steps to insure the preservation of these historic landmarks."

Rep. Raymond Anderson and Sen. R. R. Larson of Galesburg followed up this action with a measure which proposed to put all of the covered bridges squarely in the hands of the State Highway Division. This bill was also passed and it proved to be a life-saver for some of the badly deteriorating spans.

The measure, which turned the bridges over to the Highway Division, follows:

"Division 10, Department Maintenance and Control of Covered Bridges. Sec. 10-1001. The Department shall repair, maintain, operate, control and preserve every covered bridge (and the abutments and approaches thereof) in this state, meaning every structure which spans a watercourse, chasm, ravine, road or railroad in or forming a boundary line of this State and affording passage from one bank or bank thereof to the other, and which is enclosed in such manner as to prevent a clear, unimpeded view of the interior thereof from the top or longitudinal sides thereof."

The State Highway Division accepted its responsibility in stride, swinging into action immediately where help was needed the most. The measure could well set the pattern for other states, which are concerned with saving their covered bridges.

Responsibility for the various bridges was divided between several district offices operating within the Highway Division. Survey crews were sent out to the various bridges to determine just what might be needed in the way of repairs.

Much of the attention was directed to the Glenarm bridge, located 10 miles south of Springfield and almost within sight of the Illinois capital. This span was all but rebuilt after it was found in a hazardous condition. Some of the improvements included a new roof and siding, installation of abutments, new lower chords and several other changes to correct slack and sag. The total cost was $17,275 or about five times the money originally expended to build it. It is one of the best rebuilding and restoration jobs performed on covered bridges any where in the U.S.

Several other bridges came in for much attention. Roofs were replaced where needed, new floors were installed in some cases, siding was repaired and many other improvements were made.

The authentic bridges still standing include three in the northern part of the state, three in the central section and one in the southern half of the state. Two new bridges and most of the park type or private spans erected in recent years are largely confined to the northern part of the state.

Many individuals are led into this fascinating hobby by a chance crossing of a covered bridge. Such an encounter with a covered bridge is an experience which might come once in a lifetime for most. The author is one who experienced the unforgettable thrill of being introduced to covered bridges in this manner. It was actually our good fortune to encounter four of the spans this way.

The first was the Wolf bridge near Gilson and Douglas in Knox County, which was crossed on an unforgettable day in February, 1946. In the next few years in the late 1940's we experienced the rare ecstasy of such crossings on three other occasions. After crossing and re-visiting the Wolf bridge we later chanced on the Greenbush bridge in Warren county, 30 miles to the southwest. Next came the Henderson Creek span, which we discovered in a small Illinois conservation department park beside Route 164 near Oquawka. This span was not open to traffic, so we simply crossed it on foot. The fourth chance crossing was the Hamilton bridge, which at that time was serving as an approach span for highway traffic between Route 10 and the Mississippi River bridge linking Hamilton and Keokuk, IA.

The Hamilton bridge was probably the most historic span in the mid-west, serving a multitude of uses through the years before it was destroyed in a fire set by vandals on July 2, 1969. It was first a part of the Mississippi River draw span over the channel and later it was moved to the dike road where it served transcontinental auto traffic as described in the paragraph above. In more recent years it served an access road to the Montebello State Park beach area close to Hamilton.

A good starting point for a two-day or three-day tour of the covered bridges in Illinois would be the Henderson Creek bridge near Oquawka. The time required for the tour would be determined by the number of bridges you wish to visit. If you desire to tour only the historic bridges the trip could be completed in two days. However, if you wish to include several new and private bridges in your itinerary the tour would have to be stretched to three days.

You will find the restored Henderson Creek bridge in a lovely little park on the east side of Route 164 as you travel between Oquawka and Gladstone. Built in 1845 the 104-foot Burr type bridge ranks as the oldest landmark of its type in the state. It saw service at one spot on Henderson Creek for nearly a century but was apparently doomed in 1935 when construction of a new highway necessitated removal of the bridge. Residents of the area came to the rescue, however, at a meeting of the Henderson County Board, which was persuaded to rescind a previous order to dismantle the bridge. The structure was subsequently moved 200 yards upstream where it is now the center of attraction in a small park maintained by the state.

Disaster appeared to have struck the Henderson Creek bridge, also known as the Allaman span, in 1982 when it was swept downstream by a flood of record proportions. A good part of the structure was saved and a decision was made by the state agencies and community supporters to restore the bridge. The reconstructed structure was dedicated in a two-day celebration in September, 1984, with many dignitaries and upwards of 2,000 people in attendance. It was the largest covered bridge celebration in the history of the state. Two other bridge fetes in Illinois, also attended by the author, were the

100th year anniversary of the Red bridge at Princeton in 1963 and the dedication of the beautiful new Sangamon River span near Mahomet in 1964. A crowd of 300 attended the Red Bridge celebration on a rainy day and approximately 1,500 attended the Sangamon River event.

From the Henderson Creek bridge the tour would lead eastward. In other years the next stop was the Greenbush bridge in Warren County, which was destroyed by a fire bomb on the eve of Fourth of July in 1973. Efforts to restore this bridge failed despite strong community support. At one of the meetings the author presented a slide show, showing many views of several bridges in the three states which have been rebuilt or reconditioned.

A few tourists visiting the state's covered bridges still stop to view the site of the smallest covered span, and the last to be built as the covered bridge era of the nineteenth century ended. Nothing but the abutments remain.

Located a mile and a half south of Greenbush, this 58-foot bridge spanned Swan Creek, a Spoon River tributary. It was built in 1890 according to the late George Willard, whose land bordered Swan Creek. Willard recalled watching the bridge being built in that year when he was a boy 12 years old. The span was erected by a crew of three men, directed by a veteran contractor, who daily traveled the nine miles from Avon by wagon.

The Wolf bridge in adjoining Knox County would be the next objective on your tour. It is located approximately 35 miles to the northeast and could be reached from Greenbush by traveling Routes 116 and 97 and a blacktop road leading off from near the Superhighway interchange just east of Knoxville. This bridge can also be reached over three other routes, one through the town of Gilson, one through Douglas and one coming from the north alongside the east bank of Spoon River.

The Knox County Howe type span is located on the picturesque and meandering Spoon River, the stream immortalized in Edgar Lee Masters' "Spoon River Anthology." According to a plaque erected beside the bridge, it was built as an open span in 1848 and a covering was added in 1874. The bridge measures 234 feet, which includes 104 feet of the covered section and the balance in two open trestles.

The next tour objective would be the Red bridge in Bureau County, 70 miles to the northeast. This span is located a mile north of the Superhighway No. 80 interchange and a short distance west of Route 26. A Howe type span, measuring 149 feet with 95-foot approaches, it was built in 1863 in the midst of Civil war times. This is one of the most beautiful settings in Illinois. It is a photographer's and artist's delight as it lends itself to good pictures from several different points at the edge of a scenic wooded area. Photographers snap pictures from the eastern and western approaches or scramble up and down the steep banks for shots from different angles. An exceptionally magnificent view presents itself from a point 50 yards upstream where the winding creek makes a graceful swing to the east. Sand bars jutting into the stream, stretches of rock and oftentimes fishermen working the swift running water add much to the overall beauty.

No. 1 — The Red bridge near Princeton, IL.

No. 2 — Wolf bridge near Douglas and Gilson, IL.

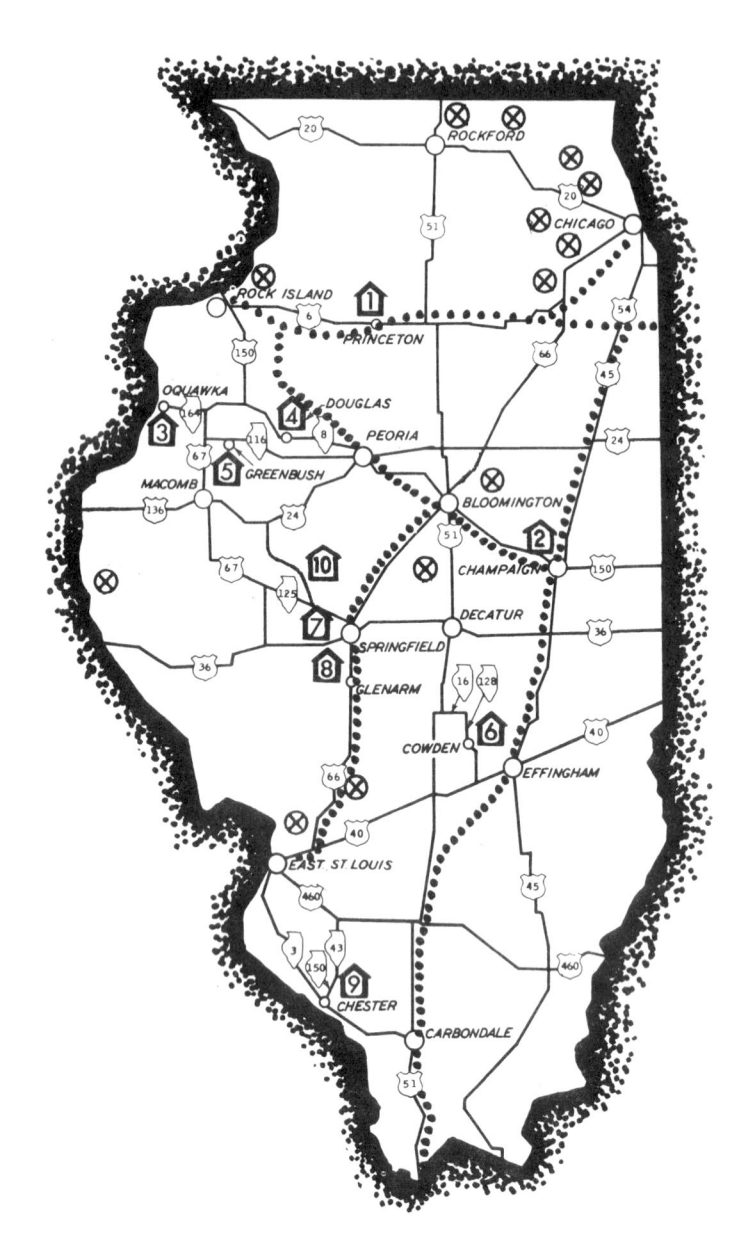

No. 3 — Illinois map of bridges, including three lost in recent decades. Dotted lines show how superhighways aid covered bridge hunting; Circled "X's" indicate some of the prominent new smaller type spans. 1) Red Bridge; 2) Sangaman River bridge; 3) Henderson Creek span; 4) Wolf bridge near Douglas and Gilson; 5) Greenbush bridge, burned in 1973; 6) Kaskaskia River bridge; 7) Spring Creek bridge, burned in 1977; 8) Glenarm span; 9) Little Mary's bridge; 10) Dismantled bridge at Petersburg.

No. 4 — Rebuilt Henderson Creek span near Oquawka, IL.

No. 5 — Greenbush bridge in Warren County, IL, burned in 1973.

No. 6 — Sangamon River bridge in Lake of Woods park.

No. 7 — Thompson Mill span on Kaskaskia River, IL.

No. 8 — Little Mary's River bridge at Chester, IL.

No. 9 — Sugar Creek bridge near Glenarm, IL.

No. 10 — Spring Creek bridge near Springfield, IL, burned in 1977.

No. 11 — Restored covered bridge at Petersburg, IL (temporarily dismantled).

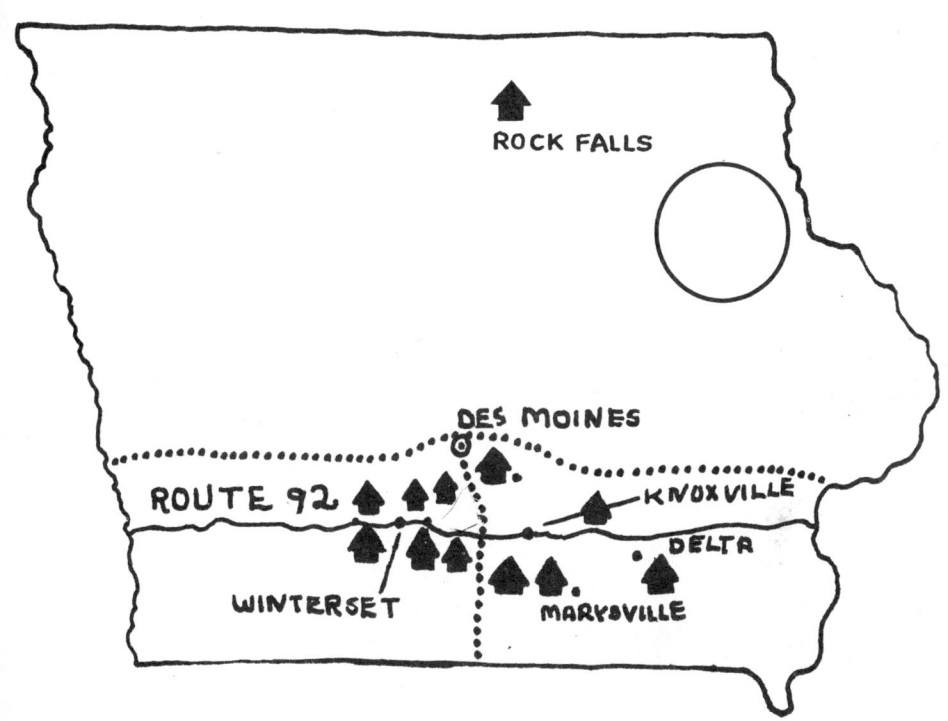

No. 12 — Iowa map of bridges. Dotted lines show how superhighways aid exploring. Circled area indicates core of "forgotten" bridges.

No. 13 — Cutler span in Winterset, IA, park.

No. 14 — McBride bridge north of Winterset, IA, burned in 1983.

No. 15 — Hogback bridge near Winterset, IA.

No. 16 — Cedar bridge near Winterset, IA.

No. 17 — Roseman bridge southwest of Winterset, IA.

No. 18 — Holliwell span southeast of Winterset, IA.

No. 19 — Imes bridge moved into St. Charles, IA.

No. 20 — North Skunk River span near Delta, IA.

No. 21 — Hammond bridge west of Marysville, IA.

No. 22 — New bridge along Shell Rock River, IA.

No. 23 — Owens bridge in Polk County, IA, park.

No. 24 — Famous span which once existed at Hamilton, IL.

No. 25 — This famous bridge was located at Boscobel, WI.

No. 26 — Mederville, IA, was the location of this famous span.

No. 27 — New bridge at State Park near Cassville, WI.

No. 28 — Red Mill bridge near Waupaca, WI.

No. 29 — Amnicon River span near Superior, WI.

No. 30 — Cedar Creek bridge near Cedarburg, WI.

No. 31 — When this Marysville, IA, bridge was dismantled in 1970 the material was converted into two smaller bridges (see next page).

How One Bridge Became Two

No. 32 — This smaller span was erected in the Wilcox Game Preserve, southeast of Knoxville, IA.

No. 33 — A view of the second bridge, which was erected in a city park at the southwest edge of Knoxville, IA.

No. 34 — New DuPage River span at Naperville. Photo by Koch.

No. 35 — Red Mill covered bridge at Waupaca. Drawing by Gloria Janetski.

If you have not lingered too long at the previously discussed bridge there would still be time in late afternoon to journey to Mahomet to visit the Sangamon River bridge, erected in 1964. Mahomet could be reached by following Route 80 to Morris and thence south on Highway 47. The Sangamon bridge is located just a short distance off the highway in a scene of much natural beauty. Tall and friendly trees bordering the Sangamon add much to the panorama.

The Sangamon was also famed in Illinois history, being mentioned often in the writings of author Masters and in Abraham Lincoln's early life. It was on the Sangamon where Lincoln made his famed raft trip which ended on a dam at the town of New Salem.

The Sangamon bridge is a 145-foot long, two-lane structure which ranks among the best covered bridges ever built in the U.S. Among its unusual features are two sidewalks four-feet wide, something almost unheard of in covered bridge construction, and rows of windows on each side. Steel and concrete provide the structural strength of the span but the upper parts are entirely of wood, preserving the traditional appearance of an old covered bridge.

The next day it would be on to Cowden, in Shelby County, 90 miles to the south where the Dry Point bridge, a structure built about 1857, crosses the Kaskaskia River.

The Kaskaskia bridge has a Howe truss and measures 160 feet with the approaches. This is one of the most scenic bridge sites in the mid-west. The river winds right up to the edge of a high wooded hill and the bridge is set flush against the steep incline on the south side. The north approach is occasionally flooded during high water periods and the only access to the site then is via a roundabout road through the rugged hill country.

Next on the tour would be the Little Mary's covered bridge in Southern Illinois in a small state picnic grounds near the City of Chester in Randolph County. This span is the last tangible link with a plank road system which once served southern Illinois and other scattered parts of the state. The plank road connected interior portions of the state with the City of Chester. It was chartered in 1853 by the state assembly.

The Little Mary's bridge was one of the first of the covered spans to be taken over by the state. It was retired in 1930 but it was preserved for posterity by the thoughtfulness of members of the Chester Chamber of Commerce, who purchased the bridge and surrounding grounds and donated them to the state. The bridge has a Burr arch truss and measures 96 feet, counting the approaches.

A covered bridge in the general area of the state capital of Springfield would be the final objective on your tour. Highway No. 4, leading out of the Chester area would take you northward to the junction with the four-lane Route 66. You would leave Highway 66 at Glenarm to visit the Sugar Creek bridge, the previously discussed rebuilt span. It is located about one and a quarter miles northwest of the town. It is a Burr type truss with a length of 111 feet.

Two other beautiful bridges in the same area around Springfield were lost from the Illinois map in the past decade. One was the Spring Creek span which was torched by vandals in 1977. The other was a "rediscovered" bridge which was dismantled after standing several years at a carriage museum near Petersburg.

This span was originally located on Horse Creek south of Springfield, west of Pawnee and not far from the town of Glenarm. It was taken out of use in 1902 when it was sold to a farmer at Pawnee where it was used as a barn and storage shed. Publicity in 1965 about the "lost" covered bridge languishing in a farm lot focused attention on the span once more. The disassembled and numbered parts of the bridge were recently donated to the Clayville Rural Life Center at Pleasant Plains for possible restoration.

This completes the tour of the major covered bridges in Illinois. If you have the time to stretch your tour there are many other covered bridges of private, semi-private or park nature which can be visited. Among them are the following:

South of Moline is a covered railroad bridge in the Niabi Zoo county park. **This is a 78-foot long span, spanning the upper end of a ravine and serving a narrow gauge railway. The bride was rebuilt and enlarged in 1985.**

Another well known private covered bridge is the Sunshine Covered Bridge in a park at the east edge of Litchfield. This 45-foot bridge could be conveniently visited on the route from the Chester to the Glenarm bridges.

At Rockton, IL, is a beautiful new covered bridge, 130 feet long spanning a well landscaped lake within the Wagon Wheel lodge grounds. This is a foot bridge which connects the lodge grounds with a convention hall.

A previously unknown Illinois covered bridge is another interesting "discovery" in recent years which eluded the census-takers. This was a 75-foot bridge, crossing Kenty Creek within the City of Rockford and serving two units of the Rockford Bolt Co. It was slated for removal almost as soon as its presence was discovered by covered-bridge lovers. But it escaped the wrecking crews when a farmer in Boone County purchased the bridge and restored it over a creek on his farm near the Winnebago-Boone County line.

Illinois is far ahead of the other states in the construction of the smaller type bridges. Many were built in the Chicago area including Cook, Lake and DuPage Counties. Nine were located in Lake County, including three added to the picturesque setting of a golf course at Vernon. Others in that county are located at Long Grove and Gurnee. Two are located in Cook County at South Barrington and Crestwood. Two of the most interesting Stringer type bridges are found in Naperville in DuPage County. One is 103 feet long and the other 83. Both are located in a Riverfront park in the downtown area.

Other new bridges are found at widely scattered points in Illinois. This group includes the following: Two at Rockford, Aurora, Dundee, Crystal Lake, Glen Carbon in Madison County, Clinton, Normal, Belvidere and Hamilton.

All of these bridges are officially recognized in the *World Guide to*

Covered Bridges. Some of the covered bridge purists have objected to mixing new smaller bridges with the sacred historic spans but the writer is happy to see them included. In this book, a covered bridge is simply that — a covered bridge.

CHAPTER IV — IOWA'S COVERED BRIDGES

Iowa's 12 covered bridges are conveniently located fairly close to broad highways and most of them are found in four closely grouped counties in the south central part of the state. The Iowa tour presents an ideal low mileage lineup for a fascinating two-day excursion. "Covered Bridge Hunting DeLuxe" might be the title of a trip to these historic structures in the heart of America.

Iowa, the great agricultural state, has gained new found importance as a covered bridge area through careful preservation of its spans during the past three decades and the recent erection of an authentic bridge in the northern part of the state.

While other states have been steadily losing these landmarks, Iowa has been tenaciously clinging to its historic mementoes, and has vaulted to 13th place in the national standings. This is a lofty spot for a state which was little known as having any covered bridges 45 to 50 years ago when the hobby of hunting them began.

There are many unusual angles to Iowa's covered bridge situation:

• Eleven of its surviving covered bridges are concentrated in a narrow 20-mile belt, extending a distance of 75 miles across the south central counties. • Only two historic spans of the state's total has been completely lost in the past 25 years.

• Six of the bridges are closely bunched in Madison County, the largest group existing in one area in the western half of the Mississippi Valley.

• Four of the Madison county bridges are of the flat-top variety, a peculiarity of this section of the mid-west.

• Iowa's spans are generally located closer to four-lane highways than those of any state in the nation.

Iowa was in the early development stage as the era of covered bridge building accompanied the west-ward push of the frontiers. When it was admitted as a state in 1846 most of the population was concentrated in the eastern one-third. The capital was then at Iowa City, only 40 miles west of the Mississippi. Most of the early spread of the population occurred across the southern half of the state, a movement which was accompanied by a slow start in the bridge building program.

Iowa's economic growth went into high gear in the post-Civil War period and most of its 85 or more covered bridges were erected from 1868 to 1880. A few were built before that era and some scattered ones were erected as late as

1890.

Two cores of covered bridge building developed in Iowa, one across about a dozen counties in the southern part of Iowa, and the other, a smaller group, in the northeastern corner of the state near the borders of Illinois, Wisconsin and Minnesota.

About 80 per cent of the spans were erected over very small rivers and creeks in the southern counties and about 15 more were erected over slightly larger streams as the Turkey, Maquoketa and Volga Rivers in "Little Switzerland," the picturesque northeastern area. More than three-fourths of the counties in Iowa were never reached by this type of timbered construction.

Iowa's early road development was slow and as late as 1846 a network of wagon trails reached only the eastern counties. In the next two decades the westward push gained momentum and stagecoach lines spread over roads which linked the growing towns. The earliest covered bridge building in Iowa coincided with the development of Fort Des Moines, a historic U.S. Army establishment at the junction of the Des Moines and Raccoon Rivers. The first was the Owens covered bridge, erected in 1844 across the North River in Polk County. A bridge was needed there in bringing in lumber for the construction of the fort. G. B. Clark was commissioned by the U.S. government to build the bridge, receiving as payment the sum of $3,500 and a half section of land. This bridge served the Dragon Trail as the road was known in those days. It was swept away in the flood of 1887. A new bridge was erected in 1887 and remained in use for more than 50 years before the road was rerouted and the channel of the river changed.

The bridge was finally taken over by the Polk County Conservation Board which moved the span in 1968 to a beautiful site in Yeader Creek Park near Des Moines where it stands today. Moving of the bridge was made necessary by the Red Rock Reservoir project, which was scheduled to flood the original site of the bridge.

Two other covered bridges were erected in the same general area near Carlisle about 1865 and both were dismantled about 1900. Some bridges were erected as far east as Winfield in Henry County, 20 miles west of the Mississippi, and others mainly in Keokuk, Tama, Lee, Marion and Madison Counties. A few other counties had one or two scattered bridges. Clayton County in the northeast had about 12 bridges, all now dismantled. Practically all of the Clayton County bridges were swept away in floods.

The construction of covered bridges reached its zenith in Madison County, a short distance to the southwest of Des Moines. Madison was not settled until 1846 but its growth was remarkable. Settling there was a group of hardy pioneers who proved to be an industrious and resourceful lot. Within the space of three decades they built a chain of saw mills and gristmills, a network of wagon trails and a series of 16 covered bridges.

The county developed at a fast pace and the bridge builders were kept busy for more than a decade erecting spans at key points. The picturesque Middle and North Rivers cut through several townships in the county and there were many places much in need of timbered construction. Wood used in the work was mostly cut by saw mills, powered by the very rivers the bridges were intended to cross. Eleven mills were erected on Middle River, which eventually was spanned by several covered bridges.

Construction actually began in 1868 when the Cox bridge was erected. Next came the Brown project, the first bridge across the North River in Jefferson Township. Both the Cox and Brown bridges were among the nine which were later razed. Then came three bridges, all erected in 1870. This group included the Imes, McBride and Cutler spans. The Year 1970 thus marked the centennial of all of these spans.

Among other bridges, erected in the county were the following: Cedar Creek, 1882, still standing; Roseman bridge, Middle River, 1883, still standing; the Adair bridge, dismantled; King bridge, Lee Township, 1877, dismantled; Cooper's Ford, Douglas township, 1878, dismantled; Backbone bridge, 1877, dismantled.

The last two covered bridges, erected in the county, both of which are still standing include the Holliwell bridge, erected over the Middle River in 1880, and the Hogback bridge over the North River in 1884. Cost of the 16 covered bridges ranged from $900 to $1,900 each. Financing was handled by a cooperative arrangement with the county board and interested landowners sharing the costs.

The development of wrought iron eventually halted erection of the wooden structures. Iron was used to some extent as early as 1872 in the construction of bridges at various points. The metal use did not completely stop wooden construction as difficulties and long delays were encountered in hauling the fabricated iron materials over oxen trails from Keokuk. The high cost of the materials, heavy transportation expenses and lack of skilled craftsmen all served to slow up metal bridge work.

After reaching their peak count of 16 in 1884, the covered bridges of Madison County gradually dwindled. One by one they disappeared as they gave way to flood, fire, vandalism and abandonment. The count had dwindled to ten in 1933 when the first protests were heard. Interested individuals gazed wistfully as the romantic links with the county's historic past vanished from the scene. Organized opposition to save the remaining ten covered bridges was begun in 1933 when the Madison County Historical Society took a hand in the situation. Heading the campaign was Mrs. Fred B. Hartsook, who took the matter direct to the county board of supervisors.

A crisis faced the covered bridges and their fate hung in the balance for several years. Long deliberations occupied the attention of the board and there was a steady parade of witnesses. While a heated controversy raged three more covered bridges were casualties. Battle lines were drawn in the county between two groups — one the history-minded citizens, who wanted the bridges preserved, and the other a combination of progress-minded people and farmers, who wanted longer, stronger and roofless spans erected. In 1950 the big decision was made. The board decided to save the remaining seven bridges. Steps were taken to repair, strengthen and paint them. Meanwhile about 30 other covered bridges were razed elsewhere in Iowa but five survivors came through to give the state a total of 12.

Few states offer all of their covered bridges in such a compact and convenient two-day tour as that which presents itself in Iowa. For sheer comfort and ease of discovery and exploration, the projected Iowa tour is unsurpassed.

Many years prior to this writing the author pointed out the odd proximity of all the 12 covered bridges to State Route 92, an old route running across the state. This geographical quirk is still evident but a new development is the east-west transcontinental four-lane Route 80 and also Route 35 traveling north and south. These two superhighways have brought all the old covered bridges in the state within 5 to 30 minutes of travelers on the nation's busiest arteries of traffic.

If you are coming from the east over Route 80 your two-day tour of Iowa's bridges might begin at Delta in Keokuk County, 25 miles south of the superhighway. The bridge will be found two miles south of town, crossing the North Skunk River. This is the oldest of the covered bridges in the state. It was erected in 1869 by Maxon Randall, a former resident of Pennsylvania, who had worked as a millwright in that state. Randall had observed covered bridge construction methods in the Quaker State, where the Burr arch truss was commonly employed. He naturally used the same type of truss in the Delta bridge. It is the only Burr arch bridge in Iowa.

The Delta bridge appeared doomed in 1955 when the abutment on one side was partly washed out by a flood on the turbulent river. When D. M. Ludwig, a Tiffin, IA, historian, called attention to the bridge's plight in the *Des Moines Register,* needed repairs were made. In recent years further work has been done on the bridge and a lovely small public park and a commemorative historical marker have been added.

Moving westward, your next objective would be three very interesting bridges, all in or near Knoxville, seat of Marion County. The most impressive is the Hammond span, a 60-foot Howe type structure found on a sylvan type road, four miles straight south of the town of Attica. Not far away was once located the Marysville covered bridge, a dilapidated structure, which appeared doomed for years. Coming to the rescue was the County Department of Conservation, which conceived the idea of dismantling the bridge and converted it in two 40-foot structures. One named the Liberty bridge, was located about 10 miles southeast of Knoxville in a game preserve area, and the other was rebuilt over a ravine in a Knoxville park.

From Knoxville the covered bridge tour would lead northwesterly to the Owens covered bridge which has been beautifully restored over the small arm of a lake in the Yeader Creek County park near the southeastern edge of Des Moines. The site is seven miles from the Owens' bridge old home over the North River near the town of Carlisle.

Next on the covered bridge tour would come the Madison County bridges. Winterset, the county seat would be the base of operations for the exciting tour coming up the next day. Arriving in Winterset in late afternoon you would find ample motel and hotel accommodations as well as camping facilities in this heart of the Iowa covered bridge country. Here you will absorb fully the flavor of an intriguing Iowa county seat town. You will have time to pick up covered bridge literature and maps at several commercial establishments and you will want to browse around in the gift shops and stores where you will find beautiful postal cards and other mementoes of your visit to the area.

Winterset is proud of its covered bridge heritage and its citizens enjoy their annual roles as hosts to thousands from all parts of the U.S. and some foreign countries. Great strides have been made by this county seat in the building of its steadily expanded tourist business. A Covered Bridge Festival, organized in 1970, draws 30,000 to 40,000 yearly.

You will thoroughly enjoy the hospitality of this busy town, which has much more than covered bridges to interest the visitors. The century-old courthouse, a remarkable building of native limestone, dominates the county square scene. Other attractions are the birthplace of John Wayne; the nearby Pammel State Park, which has a 100-foot tunneled roadway, the Old North River stone schoolhouse, built in 1874; pioneer type stone houses; and the Clark Tower.

Winterset is in a unique position with two nationally known tourist attractions in its chain of covered bridges and the Wayne home, which has been converted into a combination museum and an office by the Chamber of Commerce.

More beautiful scenery of the agricultural wonderland awaits you as you embark the next day on a fascinating 45-mile swing around the country to the covered bridges. You will never be far from Winterset as you closely follow maps, directions and many road signs erected at strategic points.

The tour of Madison County's lattice truss covered bridges could be accomplished in a half day's traveling but it is more desirable to move about at a leisurely pace in keeping with the unhurried charm of a century ago.

Many possible routs are available as you project your day's tour. You will find two of the bridges north of Route 92. A good starting point for the day's tour would be the Cedar bridge a short distance off Route 92 and close to the northeast corner of Winterset. The Cedar span is located in one of the most beautiful valleys of the county. As you come into the area from the south you follow a winding road along the bluff where a scenic panorama unfolds before you. Two routes lie ahead, one over a new highway to the right and the other over the old road to the left which still carries covered bridge visitors through the landmark. Both bridges cross meandering Cedar Creek 150 yards apart in a bowl-shaped arena, which has been converted into a park. The scene here is something of a covered bridge amphitheater spectacular. The rolling hills gently slope into the lush valley from all angles, creating a panorama seldom matched at such sites.

Next on the morning tour comes the Hogback bridge, ten miles off to the northwest and close to Winterset. The Hogback bridge, which also crosses the North River, is believed to have derived its name from a nearby ledge of rock, resembling the back of a hog. Framed by a dense woodland to the north, the Hogback provides a beautiful camera shot.

In earlier years there were two other bridges to be visited in the northern half of the county. One was the McBride bridge north of town which was arsoned in 1983 and the other was the Cutler bridge in the northeastern corner of the county, which was by-passed and moved across country to its new home in the Winterset park. It can be visited before or after swinging around to the Cedar bridge.

After lunch it is on to the Roseman bridge, nine miles southwest of Winterset. Here you will find a scene of tranquil beauty, refuting the legend that the bridge is stalked by ghosts at night. However, if you were to walk through the span alone at midnight you might sense some of the spookiness which has become associated with the bridge.

The longest bridge in Iowa comes next. It is the beautiful Holliwell bridge three miles southeast of Winterset on a gravel road to St. Charles. The Holliwell span is a 100-foot flat-top structure spanning the Middle River. The bridge is on one of the most scenic sylvan roads in the county. In early pioneer days it was the principal road linking Winterset with the southeast.

The final stop on the tour of the Madison bridges would be the Imes structure, now located at the east edge of St. Charles, just a few rods off of Superhighway 35. Before it was moved several years ago it stood in a sagging position over Clanton Creek, a small tributary of the Middle River. Extensive repairs were made to the bridge and it is now more conveniently located for the county tour.

This winds up the tour of the historical covered bridges of Iowa but the trip could be well stretched to include a 12th covered span, newly erected along the Shell Rock River near the town of Rock Falls, 125 miles north of Des Moines. This is a full scale covered bridge, copied after the Cutler span in Madison County. It was erected in 1968 by a group of public-spirited men from the Rock Falls and Plymouth communities. The road serves a well traveled graveled thoroughfare running along a scenic river.

Those who wish to dig deeper into the history of covered bridges could also visit Clayton County, 100 miles to the east, where once existed a second core of the historic spans along the Volga and Maquoketa Rivers. Nothing but a few crumpled abutments remain of the dozen or so spans in this picturesque corner of the state, which is otherwise known as "Little Switzerland." This is a land of beautiful valleys and breath-taking scenery. A bonus inducement in this area is a dozen old mills, some still functioning beside some interesting rivers. (See our book, *Old Mills in Midwest*.)

The most interesting covered bridge site is found at Mederville along the Volga River and north of Strawberry Point. Here was located the longest and highest single span covered bridge in Iowa. The bridge was a spectacular sight, measuring 255 feet across and perched about 75 to 80 feet above the water-line. Adding to the beauty of the scene was a six-story old mill, a beautiful waterfall and a boulder strewn canyon. It was erected about 1860 and was dismantled in 1918 when a new concrete and steel bridge was erected. Still standing are portions of the walls of the once lofty mill not far from the abutment of the old bridge on the west bank.

Other covered bridges in Clayton and nearby counties were located along the Volga River, or tributary creeks; some on the Milwaukee Railroad which crossed and re-crossed the winding river at several points on its torturous course; two at Otisville, one at the town of Volga City, and one at Osborne on the Elkader-Strawberry Point road. There also were two bridges on the Maquoketa River, including one wagon span eight miles southwest of Strawberry Point and another Milwaukee Railroad bridge near Worthington in Delaware County.

Most of the above bridges were destroyed by floods in the 1920's and 1930's.

If the reader wishes to expand his touring of Iowa covered bridges there are a number of new structures of the private or decorative park examples. They are found at widely scattered points in Ottumwa; Cox Creek in Clayton County; Waukee; Beaver; Waverly; and one near Fort Dodge. Practically all of these bridges were built during the wave of smaller structures which occurred during the decade of the 1970's.

CHAPTER V — WISCONSIN'S BRIDGES

Wisconsin was on the northernmost edges of the covered bridge belt as it penetrated into the mid-west and spent itself in the upper reaches of the Mississippi Valley. Much of the state was nothing more than a vast wilderness, bordering its 8,300 lakes, when covered bridge building began in other areas of the mid-west. By 1830 the population numbered only 3,245 people, who were mostly confined to the southwestern lead mining region or fur trading posts.

Growth of the state was slow and Wisconsin did not enter statehood until 1848 when most of its population was still living in the southern one-third of the territory. It was in that area that most of Wisconsin's covered bridges were built.

Wisconsin underwent a great period of development in the 1850-1890 era and its covered bridge building era, brief as it was, reached its peak in the 1870-1880 decade.

It has been variously estimated by historians and state highway commission personnel that Wisconsin once had as many as 60 of the structures. Records of many of them are lost in time but definite locations of 25 have been definitely spotted, mainly in the Wisconsin River watershed and the upper reaches of Rock River, which flows into northern Illinois.

Today there are seven covered bridges in Wisconsin, including one 19th century bridge at Cedarburg, a covered bridge of more modern vintage erected at Superior in 1926, a new covered bridge erected in 1962 in the Dewey State Park at Cassville, a new bridge erected in 1970 at Waupaca, one at the Fort Dells frontier village, one at an entrance to a country club at Mukwango, and one at the Gratiot Museum.

The Wisconsin River with its tributaries was the focal point in the early covered bridge building. Three huge covered bridges, as long as anything erected in the middle west, were built across the Wisconsin, a stream which played a vital role in the history and development of the Badger State. No history of Wisconsin could be told without frequent reference to this important stream. First came the French explorers, then the trader and trapper, then the Indian fighters, and then the pioneer settlers, who were interested in developing the area.

Several settlements began early in the 19th century and eventually a need arose for means of crossing the stream. Ferries sprang up at many key points and as trade expanded a demand for bridges was expressed. Bridging the Wisconsin was no easy task as the stream and its flood plain measured 600 to 750 feet wide in its lower reaches.

Three bridges at Portage, Boscobel and Bridgeport ranked among the costliest covered bridges ever built in the mid-west. Two of them, the 650-foot Bridgeport span and the 700-foot long Boscobel bridge are still remembered by many Wisconsin residents who crossed them as late as the 1930's, when they were finally dismantled.

A third famous Wisconsin River bridge was the Portage span, a massive three-piered structure which measured 630 feet. Erected in 1857, the Portage span was among the first covered bridges in Wisconsin. Portage had been a key point in the state's history since explorer days. It occupied a vital strip of land which bridged the Fox and Wisconsin Rivers and it is the site of a historic canal, which is still well preserved. Erected at a cost of $41,146 the Portage covered bridge served the area well for 48 years before it was demolished by a cyclone on Aug. 8, 1905. One of three sections was lifted off its piers and hurled 300 feet downstream and another section was picked up and slammed against the shoreline.

The Boscobel bridge was another famous Wisconsin structure which was regarded as an engineering triumph in its day when it was erected in 1874. The bridge was of unusual construction with a combination of wood and iron in its 700-foot length. The iron went into a 150-foot long swing section built over the Wisconsin River channel to permit passage of traffic on the then existing Great Lakes to Mississippi waterway, via the Portage canal.

The Boscobel span is remembered by the old-timers as a long, forbidding, dark and practically windowless structure. "It was really a spooky-looking place inside at night," asserted one former resident, who spent his boyhood in the area. "A sign at the entrance commanded the drivers to turn on their headlights and reduce their speed to 15 miles an hour. The children always looked forward to the trip through the tunnel as the highlight of a car trip. Sometimes children actually enjoy getting scared." The Boscobel bridge, which cost the city the sum of $45,000 was a toll span until the year 1910.

The Bridgeport bridge, located in Crawford County, 20 miles downstream from Boscobel, had a history which closely parallels the latter span. It was originally erected in 1870 to accommodate farmers on the north bank of the river, who demanded better access to the cattle shipping point of the Milwaukee railroad at Bridgeport. In later years it was sold to A. E. Lathrop, who operated it as a toll bridge until 1930. The state then paid Lathrop $15,000 for the rights to the structure, which was eventually replaced by a modern steel structure costing nearly one-half million. The Bridgeport covered span was dismantled in 1934.

The greatest concentration of covered bridges in Wisconsin was found on the Baraboo River, a tributary to the Wisconsin 80 miles upstream. Seven covered bridges were found there in Sauk County, six of them crossing the Baraboo River and one a tributary creek.

In the space of a few years the contractor Jerry Dodd and a sizeable crew of workmen erected the seven Lattice truss bridges, which were among the best known spans in Wisconsin history. This group of structures included the Butterfield span at the town of Butterfield, three at the city of Baraboo, including one near the Island Woolen mill, one connecting Ash and Walnut Streets and one on the present site of Route 12; and three others in the Ableman area, one north of that town, one near the railway station and one over Narrows Creek, west of town. Practically all of these bridges were in existence as late as the "roaring twenties," when their decline began.

The last of this group to be razed was the Butterfield bridge, which was torn down in 1934 despite some efforts to preserve it. The bridge was badly in need of repairs and much of the siding was missing. The authorities considered a proposal to save the bridge but it was finally razed when it was considered too much of a hazard to remain. It was found the public continued to use it for foot traffic and children still used it as a playground.

Other known covered bridges in Wisconsin, which have long been razed include the following:

One at Mosinee in Marathon County.

The Clarence bridge over the Sugar River between Brodhead and Juda in Green County; erected in 1867 and among the last to go about 1930.

The Ashbey bridge, erected in 1874 over the Sheboygan River on Highway 28 between Sheboygan and Kohler.

One over the Chippewa River at Chippewa Falls.

One over the Black River just below the falls near the city of Black River.

One over a creek near Orfordville in Rock County.

One over the Neshonic River at West Salem in LaCrosse County

One over the LaCrosse River north of West Salem.

One over a creek in Bloomington township in Grant County.

One over a small creek in Grant County near the Illinois-Wisconsin state line.

Two over Rock River in Beloit including the Shirland Avenue bridge and the Northwestern Railroad bridge.

One over the Kinnickinnick River on Maple Street in River Falls.

One in the vicinity of Fond du Lac near Black Wolf.

One over Rock River in the south central section of Janesville. (Erected in 1849, this may have been the first covered bridge in Wisconsin. It was razed about 1900.)

Location of the other covered bridges which served Wisconsin cannot be identified due to the lack of record-keeping before 1911 when the state highway commission was established. No records had been kept by the town and counties. Histories of the counties frequently mentioned bridges but it never occurred to the historians of that day to distinguish between open and covered spans.

By the time the commission was set up about a dozen covered bridges still remained in the state. One by one they gave way to more modern spans. A few protests were heard as the bridges were torn down but there was no organized effort to save them. Only the Cedarburg bridge, 20 miles north of Milwaukee, escaped the wrecking crews. Among the last to be razed were the Boscobel and Bridgeport spans shortly after the depression era when the nation had embarked on a broad program of road and bridge building, and other public works designed to revitalize the economic system.

A three-day tour of Wisconsin's covered bridges would take you on an unforgettable trip into an outdoor wonderland of many lakes. A good starting point might be the span erected in 1962 in the state park on Highway 133 near Cassville in the southwestern corner of the state. The 50-foot bridge, which spans Dewey Creek, is located at the entrance to the Stonefield Village, a recreated settlement of 20 shops and buildings of the "gay nineties" era.

Here you will board a horse-drawn wagon-type omnibus and absorb the full flavor of the "good old days," experiencing the rare thrill of crossing a covered bridge with two horses supplying the motive power. You will hear the rumble of the wheels and the heavy hooves going clippity clop as the team plods across the planks. As you emerge from the bridge the fascinating scene of an old time town unfolds before you.

The span is believed to be the first bridge completely pre-fabricated in another state and reassembled at its permanent site. The parts for the Howe type truss were made at the Wheeler Construction Co. in Minnesota, shipped to Cassville by rail and assembled at the park by the Grant County Highway

Department, the Wisconsin Conservation Department and the State Historical Society.

Also in the southwestern corner of Wisconsin is a 50-foot Stringer type of bridge at the Fox Museum at Gratiot, not far from the Illinois-Wisconsin boundary. In other years the Wisconsin tour included an interesting covered span at the city of Richland Center. This was a home town development project over a small creek. After several years of service it was finally dismantled owing to weight limitations.

It is doubtful that any covered bridge ever had its inception just like the Richland Center project. Back in 1967 the Junior Chamber of Commerce was casting about, looking for something new in the way of a worthwhile community project. One of the members noticed a news item from another town, which told of an unsuccessful attempt to build a covered bridge over a state highway.

"Why can't we build one here?" one of the members asked. The idea caught on immediately and the following spring the members of the chamber rolled up their sleeves and erected a creditable covered bridge, despite a complete lack of experience in such work. The project attracted nation-wide attention and it reached all the way to Washington. When the structure was dedicated, participating in the ceremonies were the two daughters of President Richard Nixon.

The legend on the plaque over the bridge's entrance reads:

JAYCEE COVERED BRIDGE
In appreciation of county residents' support of all
JC projects, we dedicate this bridge
David Froh, president
Bernard Standele, township chairman
Dedicated on this day, July 12, 1868 by
Julie and Trisha Nixon

From southwest Wisconsin the route would lead to the Wisconsin Dells where you will find a beautiful covered bridge at Fort Dells, an authentic replica of a frontier fort with many side features. The bridge is a good-sized replica, about 35 feet long and located in a tree-shrouded scenic area. Other attractions here are a swaying suspension bridge, a frontier town, a children's farm, a paddle wheel steamer and many other features.

In the vicinity of the Dells many side trips are available to nationally historic places. The principal spots are the historic canal at Portage; the Surgeons' Quarters at the site of Fort Winnebago and the old Indian Agency House also at Portage; the world reknown Circus Museum at Baraboo and the Mid-Continent Railway Museum at North Freedom.

After leaving the Dells the next stop would be the beautiful Red Mill covered bridge three miles south of Waupaca on Highway K. This is an authentic Town truss type of span over the Crystal River. Visitors here will have an opportunity to visit also the Red Mill, which is listed in the book, *Old Mills in the Mid-West*, as one of the top eight attrations of this type in the state. The 40-foot bridge was built by local craftsmen in 1970. Forty-foot lengths of lumber were transported all the way from Oregon and 400 hand-made wooden tree nails were pounded into the structure. This bridge was patterned after one of a similar type in New Hampshire. A Chapel in the Woods on the Mill property is another feature to interest visitors here.

While in the Waupaca area visitors might also visit two smaller covered bridges including one over the Waupaca River at the west end of Waupaca and another over a branch of the Crystal River in the Village of Rural.

Other small bridges in Wisconsin not previously mentioned include spans at Broadhead, Sparta, one near West Bend, one in Crawford County and a series of several small structures on trail ride routes in Marinette County.

The tour would next lead you to the north over well traveled highways to the Superior area at the western tip of Lake Superior. There you will find a delightful bridge spanning the beautiful Amnicon River which falls and tumbles toward the lake through some of the most spectacular scenery in northern Wisconsin.

The river sweeps over three falls of about 30 feet each and further drops in a series of cascades and rapids which the bridge spans. In the succession of falls and rapids the river descends 175 feet within the mile and a half which it courses through the park. After a rainstorm the white water cascading through the gorge and rushing against the rocks provides even more breath-taking scenery. It is a spectacular setting for a covered bridge. The span, which is used only as a foot bridge, was originally located over the Pokegama River near the entrance to Graceland Cemetery about a mile southwest of Superior. In 1926 the bridge was removed and reassembled at the Amnicon site, being replaced by a heavier span. It was once used to convey traffic over the Pokegama but at the Amnicon site it serves only pedestrians. It was originally built as an open span but a covering was added in 1938 by the town of Amnicon for the double purpose of protecting the bridge and providing a shelter for visitors during inclement weather. The bridge is 56 feet long and 18 feet wide with a pony truss and through arch chord.

The next stop on the Wisconsin tour would be the Cedarburg covered bridge over Cedar Creek, three miles north of the city of Cedarburg, only five miles away from Lake Michigan. The Cedarburg span is Wisconsin's last survivor of its 19th century bridge building era.

A town lattice type structure 120 feet long, it was erected in 1876 and served the community faithfully until 1962, when it began a life of semi-retirement. The bridge was taken out of service after the completion of a modern type span just a few feet away. The new bridge is an open type structure with wooden railings and posts, designed to blend harmoniously with the historic span beside it.

A small park has been set up in the area surrounding the historic bridge which is conveniently located near the junction of the Routes 60 and 143 on the Covered Bridge Road. On May 23, 1865 the site was commemorated with a

State Historical Society Official Marker which follows:

LAST COVERED BRIDGE

Built 1878   Retired 1962

This bridge was built by the Town of Cedarburg on Petition of neighboring farmers to replace periodically washed out bridges. Pine logs, cut and milled at Baraboo, were fitted and set in place in lattice truss construction with 3x6 inch planks secured by 2-inch hardwood pins, eliminating the use of nails or bolts, and floored by 3-inch planking. The Ozaukee County Board in 1940 voted to assume the preservation and maintenance of the bridge.

Erected 1965

Ozaukee County Historical Society

This would conclude the tour of bridges in the tri-state area. As you finish this tour you will come away with the rewarding feeling of having stepped back into time, re-living a period of yesteryear when life moved at a much slower tempo. If it is your first visit to the covered bridge country you will feel you have had an unforgettable experience. You will also feel you will want to tour the area again some day and perhaps visit covered bridges in other states.

Author's notes: *Our files include extra photographs and some postal cards of the bridges shown in this book. Extra copies of this book are available at $4 a copy. Write to:* **Leslie Swanson, P.O. Box 334, Moline, IL 61265.** *(Circular on other covered bridge books free on request. Please send stamped self-addressed envelope.)*

BOOKS ON AMERICANA

by

Leslie Swanson

CANALS OF MID-AMERICA— The romantic small canals of history as they look today. The Old Towpath, rediscovered by hobbyists in many fields. Resurgence of interest. The Great Canal Corridor set up. Four new authentic canal boats draw tourists. 52 pages, 22 illustrations. Price $3.00.

RURAL ONE-ROOM SCHOOLS— A fascinating story of education in the rural areas before consolidation. The romance of the "Little Red Schoolhouse." How the teachers carried torch of learning to the farm youths. New drive to save buildings. 40 pages, 23 illustrations. $3.00.

STEAMBOAT CALLIOPES— The enchanting music of the early day steam pianos on excursion boats and modern day craft such as the Queens. Invented in Vermont, first used on Hudson River. From the "Roaring Twenties" to present day use. 50 pages, 22 illustrations. $3.00.

OLD MILLS IN THE MID-WEST— The old time water wheels of history. A colorful era of America's past. How many survive in preservation projects. Chapters on famed mills at Hinsdale and Pine Creek. History of milling since ancient times. 42 pages, 20 illustrations. $3.00.

Address Author, Leslie Swanson, P.O. Box 334, Moline, IL 61265